Hidden Treasure
Memorizing God's Word
for Children

and

BIBLE STUDY ANSWERS
Using the King James Version

Compiled by Nancy Dunnewin

TEACH Services, Inc.
PUBLISHING
www.TEACHServices.com • (800) 367-1844

World rights reserved. This book or any portion thereof may not be copied or reproduced in any form or manner whatever, except as provided by law, without the written permission of the publisher, except by a reviewer who may quote brief passages in a review.

The author assumes full responsibility for the accuracy of all facts and quotations as cited in this book. The opinions expressed in this book are the author's personal views and interpretations, and do not necessarily reflect those of the publisher.

This book is provided with the understanding that the publisher is not engaged in giving spiritual, legal, medical, or other professional advice. If authoritative advice is needed, the reader should seek the counsel of a competent professional.

Copyright © 2023 TEACH Services, Inc.
ISBN-13: 978-1-4796-1535-3 (Paperback)
ISBN-13: 978-1-4796-1537-7 (Spiral)
ISBN-13: 978-1-4796-1536-0 (ePub)
Library of Congress Control Number: 2022922888

All Bible verse references are from the King James Version (KJV) of the Bible. Public domain. Underline emphasis provided by author.

Copyrighted artwork used by permission from Feeding His Lambs Ministries.

Published by

www.TEACHServices.com • (800) 367-1844

Table of Contents

BIBLE STUDY TOPIC

1. Can We Trust the Bible? 8
2. Origin of Sin 10
3. Salvation 12
4. Heaven and New Earth 14
5. God's Law 16
6. Sabbath 18
7. How to Keep the Sabbath 20
8. First Day 22
9. Signs of Jesus' Coming 24
10. Second Coming 26
11. Baptism 28
12. Prophecy 30
13. Health 32
14. Tithes and Offerings 34
15. Sanctuary 36
16. Judgment 38
17. Church Standards 40
18. Death 42
19. 1,000 Years 44
20. The Little Horn 46
21. Mark of the Beast 48
22. Three Angels' Messages 50
23. Seven Last Plagues 52
24. Trust and Obey 54
25. True Church 56

BIBLE STUDY ANSWERS 59
Can We Trust The Bible? 60
Origin of Sin 61
Salvation 62
Heaven And New Earth 63
God's Law 64
Sabbath 65
How to Keep the Sabbath 66
First Day 67
Signs of Jesus' Coming 68
Second Coming 69
Baptism 70
Prophecy 71
Health 72
Tithes and Offerings 73
Sanctuary 74
Judgment 75
Church Standards 76
Death 77
1,000 Years 78
The Little Horn 79
Mark of the Beast 80
Three Angels' Messages 81
Seven Last Plagues 82
Trust And Obey 83
True Church 84

Hidden Treasures

Memorizing God's Word

This book of Bible studies is designed to encourage you to memorize God's Word. Take God's Word and study it, memorize it as if looking for hidden treasure.

These Bible studies with their Bible answers use the first two words of the verse and the first letter of each subsequent word, which helps to memorize God's Word. The complete Bible study answers are at the end of this book.

"Jesus saith u h, I a t w, t t, a t l: n m c u t F, b b m."

"Jesus saith unto him, I am the way, the truth, and the life;
no man cometh unto the Father, but by me."
John 14:6

1
CAN WE TRUST THE BIBLE?

1. What did Jesus say about Himself? John 14:6

2. What is truth? John 17:17

3. Is Scripture inspired? 2 Timothy 3:16

4. Where did Scripture come from? 2 Peter 1:21

5. What should we do with God's Word? Psalm 119:11

6. What is God's Word to us? Psalm 119:105

Lesson 1

1. John 14:6	Jesus saith u h, I a t w, t t, a t l: n m c u t F, b b m.
2. John 17:17	Sanctify them t t t: t w i t.
3. 2 Timothy 3:16	All Scripture i g b i o G, a i p f d, f r, f c, f i i r
4. 2 Peter 1:21	For the p c n i o t b t w o m: b h m o G s a t w m b t H G.
5. Psalm 119:11	Thy word h I h i m h t I m n s a t.
6. Psalm 119:105	Thy word i a l u m f, a a l u m p.

(Bible Study Answers can be found starting on page 60.)

CAN WE TRUST THE BIBLE?

2
ORIGIN OF SIN

1. Why is there sin? I John 3:8

2. Who did Lucifer want to be like? Isaiah 14:12–14

3. What happened to Lucifer in heaven? Revelation 12:9

4. What is sin? 1 John 3:4

5. How many have sinned? Romans 3:23

6. Is there hope for sinners? John 3:16

Lesson 2

1. I John 3:8	He that c s i o t d; f t d s f t b.
2. Isaiah 14:12–14	How art t f f h, O L, s o t m! ... F t h s i t h ... I w b l t m H.
3. Revelation 12:9	And the g d w c o, t o s, c t D, a S, w d t w w: h w c o i t e, a h a w c o w h.
4. 1 John 3:4	Whosoever committeth s t a t l: f s i t t o t l.
5. Romans 3:23	For all h s, a c s o t g o G.
6. John 3:16	For God s l t w, t h g h o b S, t w b i h s n p, b h e l.

ORIGIN OF SIN

3

SALVATION

1. What question did the jailer ask? Acts 16:30

2. What must we do to be saved? Acts 16:31

3. What are the wages of sin and the gift of God? Romans 6:23

4. What happens when we confess our sins? 1 John 1:9

5. Why did Jesus die for us? John 3:16

6. What is Jesus saying to you today? Revelation 3:20

Lesson 3

1. Acts 16:30	And brought t o, a s, S, w m I d t b s?
2. Acts 16:31	And they s, B o t L J C, a t s b s, a t h.
3. Romans 6:23	For the w o s i d; b t g o G i e l t J C o L.
4. 1 John 1:9	If we c o s, h i f a j t f u o s, a t c u f a u.
5. John 3:16	For God s l t w, t h g h o b S, t w b i h s n p, b h e l.
6. Revelation 3:20	Behold, I s a t d, a k: i a m h m v, a o t d, I w c i t h, a w s w h, a h w m.

SALVATION 13

4

HEAVEN AND NEW EARTH

1. Is there a heaven? John 14:2–3

2. Who knows what God has prepared for us? 1 Corinthians 2:9

3. What did John the Revelator see? Revelation 21:2, 4

4. What else has God prepared? Revelation 22:2

5. What will we do in the New Earth? Isaiah 65:21

6. Who will have the right to all of this? Revelation 22:14

Lesson 4

1. John 14:2–3	In my F h a m m: i i w n s, I w h t y. I g t p a p f y. A i I g a p a p f y, I w c a, a r y u m; t w I a, t y m b a.
2. 1 Corinthians 2:9	But as i i w, E h n s, n e h, n h e i t h o m, t t w G h p f t t l h.
3. Revelation 21:2, 4	And I J s t h c, n J, c d f G o o h, p a a b a f h h … A G s w a a t f t e; a t s b n m d, n s, n c, n s t b a m p: f t f t a p a
4. Revelation 22:2	In the m o t s o i, a o e s o t r, w t t t o l, w b t m o f.
5. Isaiah 65:21	And they s b h, a i t; a t s p v, a e t f o t.
6. Revelation 22:14	Blessed are t t d h c, t t m h r t t t o l, a m e i t t g i t c.

HEAVEN AND NEW EARTH 15

5

GOD'S LAW

1. Is God's law good? Romans 7:12

2. What is man's responsibility to God? Ecclesiastes 12:13

3. Did Jesus change the law? Matthew 5:17

4. Can we throw away any part of the Bible? James 2:10

5. How long will God's law endure? Psalm 111:7–8

6. How does God know we love Him? John 14:15

Lesson 5

1. Romans 7:12	Wherefore the l i h, a t c h, a j, a g.
2. Ecclesiastes 12:13	Let us h t c o t w m: F G, a k h c: f t i t w d o m.
3. Matthew 5:17	Think not t I a c t d t l, o t p: I a n c t d, b t f.
4. James 2:10	For whosoever s k t w l, a y o i o p, h i g o a.
5. Psalm 111:7–8	The works o h h a v a j; a h c a s. T s f f e a e, a a d i t a u.
6. John 14:15	If ye l m, k m c.

GOD'S LAW

6
SABBATH

1. What did God do after creating the world? Genesis 2:3

2. Did God mention the Sabbath in His Commandments? Exodus 20:8

3. On what day did Jesus worship? Luke 4:16

4. What day of the week did Jesus' followers keep holy? Luke 23:56

5. Will Sabbath be kept in heaven? Isaiah 66:23

6. Who was the Sabbath made for? Mark 2:27–28

Lesson 6

1. Genesis 2:3	And God b t s d, a s i: b t i i h h r f a h w w G c a m.
2. Exodus 20:8	Remember the s d, t k i h.
3. Luke 4:16	And He c t N, w h h b b u: a, a h c w, h w i t s o t s d, a s u f t r.
4. Luke 23:56	And they r, a p s a o; a r t s d a t t c.
5. Isaiah 66:23	And it s c t p, t f o n m t a, a f o s t a, s a f c t w b m, s t L
6. Mark 2:27–28	And he s u t, T s w m f m, a n m f t s: T t S o m i L a o t s.

SABBATH 19

7
HOW TO KEEP THE SABBATH

1. What did Jesus say about the Sabbath? Exodus 20:8–11

2. What is the preparation day? Mark 15:42

3. How long was each day of creation? Genesis 1:5

4. How do we keep the Sabbath holy? Isaiah 58:13

5. Should we help others on Sabbath? Matthew 12:12

6. Why is Sabbath observance so important? Ezekiel 20:20

Lesson 7

1. Exodus 20:8–11	Remember the s d, t k i h. S d s t l, a d a t w: B t s d i t s o t L t G: i i t s n d a w, t, n t s, n t d, t m, n t m, n t c, n t s t i w t g: F i s d t L m h a e, t s, a a t i t i, a r t s d: w t L b t s d, a h i.
2. Mark 15:42	And now w t e w c, b i w t p, t i, t d b t s.
3. Genesis 1:5	And the e a t m w t f d.
4. Isaiah 58:13	If thou t a t f f t s, f d t p o m h d; a c t s a d, t h o t L, h; a s h h, n d t o w, n f t o p, n s t o w.
5. Matthew 12:12	Wherefore it i l t d w o t s d.
6. Ezekiel 20:20	And hallow m s; a t s b a s b m a y, t y m k t I a t L y G.

HOW TO KEEP THE SABBATH

21

8
FIRST DAY

1. What does Matthew say about the first day? Matthew 28:1

2. What does Mark say about the first day? Mark 16:2

3. What does Luke say about the first day? Luke 24:1

4. What does John say about the first day? John 20:1

5. What did God do on the first day of creation? Genesis 1:5

6. Why do most people worship on Sunday? Matthew 15:9

Lesson 8

1. Matthew 28:1	In the e o t s, a i b t d t t f d o t w, c M M a t o M t s t s.
2. Mark 16:2	And very e i t m t f d o t w, t c u t s a t r o t s.
3. Luke 24:1	Now upon t f d o t w, v e i t m, t c u t s, b t s w t h p, a c o w t.
4. John 20:1	The first d o t w c M M e, w i w y d, u t s, a s t s t a f t s.
5. Genesis 1:5	And God c t l D, a t d h c N. A t e a t m w t f d.
6. Matthew 15:9	But in v t d w m, t f d t c o m.

FIRST DAY

9

SIGNS OF JESUS' COMING

1. What are some signs of Jesus' coming? Matthew 24:7

2. What will people be like in the last days? 2 Timothy 3:2–3

3. Will there be signs in our own galaxy? Matthew 24:29

4. Will there be a time of trouble? Matthew 24:21

5. What is the last prophecy to be fulfilled? Matthew 24:14

6. What will be the final event? Matthew 24:30

Lesson 9

1. Matthew 24:7	For nation s r a n, a k a k: a t s b f, a p, a e, i d p.
2. 2 Timothy 3:2–3	For men s b l o t o s, c, b, p, b, d t p, u, u, W n a, t, f a, i, f, d o t t a g.
3. Matthew 24:29	Immediately after t t o t d s t s b d, a t m s n g h l, a t s s f f h, a t p o t h s b s.
4. Matthew 24:21	For then s b g t, s a w n s t b o t w t t t, n, n e s b.
5. Matthew 24:14	And this g o t k s b p i a t w f a w u a n; a t s t e c.
6. Matthew 24:30	And then s a t s o t S o m i h: a t s a t t o t e m, a t s s t S o m c i t c o h w p a g g.

SIGNS OF JESUS' COMING

10

THE SECOND COMING

1. What promise did Jesus give? John 14:2–3

2. How did Jesus go back to heaven? Acts 1:11

3. Who will see Jesus return? Revelation 1:7

4. When should we get ready for Jesus' return? Matthew 24:44

5. What should we do when we see the signs of Jesus' coming? Luke 21:28

6. When will He return? Matthew 24:36

Lesson 10

1. John 14:2–3	In my F h a m m: i i w n s, I w h t y. I g t p a p f y. A i I g a p a p f y, I w c a, a r y u m; t w I a, t y m b a.
2 Acts 1:11	This same J, w i t u f y i h, s s c i l m a y h s h g i h.
3. Revelation 1:7	Behold He c w c; a e e s s h.
4. Matthew 24:44	Therefore be y a r: f i s a h a y t n t S o m c.
5. Luke 21:28	And when t t b t c t p, t l u, a l u y h; f y r d n.
6. Matthew 24:36	But of t d a h k n m, n, n t a o h, b m F o.

THE SECOND COMING 27

11
BAPTISM

1. Does God require baptism? Mark 16:16

2. How many kinds of baptism are there? Ephesians 4:5

3. How did Philip baptize the eunuch? Acts 8:37–38

4. What did Jesus do about baptism? Mark 1:9–11

5. Why was Jesus baptized? 1 Peter 2:21

6. What great commission has the Lord given us? Matthew 28:19–20

Lesson 11

1. Mark 16:16	He that b a i b s b s; b h t b n s b d.
2. Ephesians 4:5	One Lord, o f, o b.
3. Acts 8:37–38	And Philip s, I t b w a t h, t m. A h a a s, I b t J C i t S o G. A h c t c t s s: a t w d b i t w, b P a t e; a h b h.
4. Mark 1:9–11	And it c t p it d, t J c f N o G, a w b o J i J. A s c u o o t w, h s t h o, a t S l a d d u h: A t c a v f h, s, T a m b S, i w I a w p.
5. 1 Peter 2:21	For even h w y c: b C a s f u, l u a e, t y s f h s.
6. Matthew 28:19–20	Go ye t, a t a n, b t i t n o t F, a o t S, a o t H G: T t t o a t w I h c y: a, l, I a w y a, e u t e o t w. A.

BAPTISM

29

12
PROPHECY

1. What is the true church going to have? Revelation 12:17

2. What is the testimony of Jesus? Revelation 19:10

3. Whom does God use? 2 Peter 1:21

4. Through whom does God reveal things? Amos 3:7

5. What is the test of a true prophet? Isaiah 8:20

6. Will we have prophets in the last days? Acts 2:17

Lesson 12

1. Revelation 12:17	And the d w w w t w, a w t m w w t r o h s, w k t c o G, a h t t o J C.
2. Revelation 19:10	And I f a h f t w h. A h s u m, S t d i n: I a t f s, a o t b t h t t o J: w G: f t t o J i t s o p.
3. 2 Peter 1:21	For the p c n i o t b t w o m: b h m o G s a t w m b t H G.
4. Amos 3:7	Surely the L G w d n, b h r h s u h s t p.
5. Isaiah 8:20	To the l a t t t: i t s n a t t w, i i b t i n l i t.
6. Acts 2:17	And it s c t p it l d, s G, I w p o o m S u a f: a y s a y d s p, a y y m s s v, a y o m s d d.

13
HEALTH

1. What was man's original diet? Genesis 1:29

2. When did man start eating vegetables? Genesis 3:18

3. When did man begin to eat meat? Genesis 9:3

4. How many of each animal was spared in the flood? Genesis 7:2

5. Is all meat clean? Deuteronomy 14:3, 6, 9

6. Does it matter what we eat and drink? 1 Corinthians 10:31

Lesson 13

1. Genesis 1:29	And God s, B, I h g y e h b s, w i u t f o a t e, a e t, i t w i t f o a t y s; t y i s b f m.
2. Genesis 3:18	Thorns also a t s i b f t t; a t s e t h o t f.
3. Genesis 9:3	Every moving t t l s b m f y; e a t g h h I g y a t.
4. Genesis 7:2	Of every c b t s t t t b s, t m a h f: a o b t a n c b t, t m a h f.
5. Deuteronomy 14:3, 6, 9	Thou shalt n e a a t. ... A e b t p t h, a c t c i t c, a c t c a t b, t y s e. ...... T y s e o a t a i t w: a t h f a s s y e.
6. 1 Corinthians 10:31	Whether therefore y e, o d, o w y d, d a t t g o G.

HEALTH 33

14

TITHES AND OFFERINGS

1. Who owns everything? Psalm 24:1

2. Where should our treasure be stored? Matthew 6:20–21

3. What is tithe? Leviticus 27:32

4. What promise comes with paying tithe? Malachi 3:10

5. What else can we give besides tithe? Psalm 96:8

6. How does God want us to give? 2 Corinthians 9:7

Lesson 14

1. Psalm 24:1	The earth i t L, a t f t; t w, a t t d t.
2. Matthew 6:20–21	But lay u f y t i h, w n m n r d c, a w t d n b t n s: F w y t i, t w y h b a.
3. Leviticus 27:32	And concerning t t o t h, o o t f, e o w p u t r, t t s b h u t L.
4. Malachi 3:10	Bring ye a t t i t s, t t m b m i m h, a p m n h, s t L o h, i I w n o y t w o h, a p y o a b, t t s n b r e t r i.
5. Psalm 96:8	Give unto t L t g d u h n: b a o, a c i h c.
6. 2 Corinthians 9:7	Every man a a h p i h h, s l h g; n g, o o n: f G l a c g

TITHES AND OFFERINGS 35

15

SANCTUARY

1. Why did God tell Moses to build a sanctuary? Exodus 25:8

2. Describe the sanctuary. Hebrews 9:2–3

3. How were sins forgiven at that time? Leviticus 4:29

4. Who is the True Lamb? John 1:29

5. What did the Old Testament sanctuary represent? Hebrews 9:24

6. How are sins forgiven today? Acts 4:12

Lesson 15

1. Exodus 25:8	And let t m m a s; t I m d a t.
2. Hebrews 9:2–3	For there w a t m; t f, w w t c, a t t, a t s; w i c t s. A a t s v, t t w i c t H o a.
3. Leviticus 4:29	And he s l h h u t h o t s o, a s t s o i t p o t b o.
4. John 1:29	The next d J s J c u h, a s, B t L o G, w t a t s o t w.
5. Hebrews 9:24	For Christ i n e i t h p m w h, w a t f o t t; b i h i, n t a i t p o G f u.
6. Acts 4:12	Neither is t s i a o: f t i n o n u h g a m, w w m b s.

SANCTUARY

37

16
JUDGMENT

1. Who will be judged? Ecclesiastes 3:17

2. Does God have a record of our lives? Ecclesiastes 12:14

3. What method does God use to judge? Revelation 20:12

4. How many will be judged? 2 Corinthians 5:10

5. Are we held accountable for our actions? Romans 14:12

6. How is God's reward distributed? Revelation 22:12

Lesson 16

1. Ecclesiastes 3:17	I said i m h, G s j t r a t w: f t i a t t f e p a f e w.
2. Ecclesiastes 12:14	For God s b e w i j, w e s t, w i b g, o w i b e.
3. Revelation 20:12	And I s t d, s a g, s b G; a t b w o: a a b w o, w i t b o l: a t d w j o o t t w w w i t b, a t t w.
4. 2 Corinthians 5:10	For we m a a b t j s o C.
5. Romans 14:12	So then e o o u s g a o h t G.
6. Revelation 22:12	And, behold, I c q; a m r i w m, t g e m a a h w s b.

JUDGMENT

17
CHURCH STANDARDS

1. What principle should guide the Christian at all times? Philippians 4:8

2. Should God be glorified in every aspect of our lives? 1 Corinthians 10:31

3. What is God's advice to us? Ephesians 4:31–32

4. Is God concerned with the words we speak? Ephesians 5:4

5. How can a Christian avoid being worldly? Romans 12:2

6. What high standard should we have regarding jewelry? 1 Peter 3:3

Lesson 17

1. Philippians 4:8	Finally, brethren, w t a t, w t a h, w t a j, w t a p, w t a l, w t a o g r; i t b a v, a i t b a p, t o t t.
2. 1 Corinthians 10:31	Whether therefore y e, o d, o w y d, d a t t g o G.
3. Ephesians 4:31–32	Let all b, a w, a a, a c, a e s, b p a f y, w a m: A b y k o t a, t, f o a, e a G f C s h f y.
4. Ephesians 5:4	Neither filthiness, n f t, n j, w a n c: b r g o t.
5. Romans 12:2	And be n c t t w: b b y t b t r o y m, t y m p w i t g, a a, a p, w o G.
6. 1 Peter 3:3	Whose adorning l i n b t o a o p t h, a o w o g, o o p o o a.

CHURCH STANDARDS 41

18
DEATH

1. What warning did God give Adam & Eve? Genesis 2:17

2. What lie did the serpent tell Eve? Genesis 3:4

3. What happens to our bodies at death? Ecclesiastes 12:7

4. What is man's spirit, according to the Bible? Job 27:3

5. How did God make man? Genesis 2:7

6. Will the dead live again? John 5:28–29

Lesson 18

1. Genesis 2:17	But of t t o t k o g a e, t s n e o i: f i t d t t e t t s s d.
2. Genesis 3:4	And the s s u t w, y s n s d.
3. Ecclesiastes 12:7	Then shall t d r t t e a i w: a t s s r u G w g i.
4. Job 27:3	All the w m b i i m, a t s o G i i m n.
5. Genesis 2:7	And the L G f m o t d o t g, a b i h n t b o l; a m b a l s.
6. John 5:28–29	Marvel not a t: f t h i c, i t w a t a i t g s h h v, A s c f; t t h d g, u t r o l; a t t h d e, u t r o d.

DEATH

19

1,000 YEARS

1. What happens to the devil at Christ's coming? Revelation 20:1–2

2. What happens to the righteous during the thousand years? Revelation 20:6

3. What will the righteous do during the millennium? Revelation 20:4

4. What is earth like during the millennium? Jeremiah 4:23

5. How does Jesus cleanse the earth? Revelation 20:7–10

6. What about God's children during and after the millennium (one thousand years)? Revelation 21:4

Lesson 19

1. Revelation 20:1–2	And I s a a c d f h, h t k o t b p a a g c i h h. A h l h o t d, t o s, w i t D, a S, a b h a t y.
2. Revelation 20:6	Blessed and h i h t h p i t f r: o s t s d h n p, b t s b p o G a o C, a s r w h a t y.
3. Revelation 20:4	And I s t, a t s u t, a j w g u t … a t l a r w C a t y.
4. Jeremiah 4:23	I beheld t e, a, l, i w w f, a v; a t h, a t h n l.
5. Revelation 20:7, 10	And when t t y a e, S s b l o o h p, … A t d t d t w c i t l o f a b.
6. Revelation 21:4	And God s w a a t f t e; a t s b n m d, n s, n c, n s t b a m p: f t f t a p a.

20

THE LITTLE HORN

1. What four beasts did Daniel see? Daniel 7:4–7

2. What did they represent? Daniel 7:17

3. What was the little horn to do? Daniel 7:8

4. What is blasphemy? Mark 2:7

5. How does John describe blasphemy? John 10:33

6. What does the little horn try to do to God's law? Daniel 7:25

Lesson 20

1. Daniel 7:4–7	*First beast*—The first w l a l, a h e w. *Second beast*—And behold a b, a s, l t a b. *Third beast*—After this I b, a l a, l a l. *Fourth beast*—After this I s i t n v, b a f b, d a t, a s e; a i h g i t.
2. Daniel 7:17	These great b, w a f, a f k, w s a o o t e.
3. Daniel 7:8	I considered t h, a, b, t c u a t a l h … a, b, i t h w e l t e o m, a a m s g t.
4. Mark 2:7	Why doth t m t s b? w c f s b G o?
5. John 10:33	The Jews a h, s, F a g w w s t n; b f b; a b t t, b a m, m t G.
6. Daniel 7:25	And he s s g w a t m H, a s w o t s o t m H, a t t c t a l: a t s b g i h h u a t a t a t d o t.

THE LITTLE HORN

21

MARK OF THE BEAST

1. Where in the Bible is the seal of God found? Exodus 20:8, 11

2. Why do we keep the Sabbath? Exodus 31:17

3. Who are the children of Israel? Galatians 3:26, 29

4. What are the two great powers? Revelation 12:17

5. Who is the beast power? Revelation 13:2

6. Where is the mark of the beast found? Revelation 13:16

Lesson 21

1. Exodus 20:8, 11	Remember the s d, t k i h .... F i s d t L m h a e, t s, a a t i t i, a r t s d: w t L b t s d, a h i.
2. Exodus 31:17	It is a s b m a t c o I f e: f i s d t L m h a e, a o t s d h r, a w r.
3. Galatians 3:26, 29	For ye a a t c o G b f i C J .... A i y b C, t a y A s, a h a t t p.
4. Revelation 12:17	And the d w w w t w, a w t m w w t r o h s, w k t c o G, a h t t o J C.
5. Revelation 13:2	And the b w I s w l u a l, a h f w a t f o a b, a h m a t m o a l: a t d g h h p, a h s, a g a.
6. Revelation 13:16	And he c a, b s a g, r a p, f a b, t r a m i t r h, o i t f.

48

MARK OF THE BEAST 49

22

THREE ANGELS' MESSAGES

1. What is the first angel's message? Revelation 14:7

2. What is the second angel's message? Revelation 14:8

3. What is Babylon? Revelation 18:2

4. What is the third angel's message? Revelation 14:9–10

5. Who gets victory over the beast? Revelation 14:12

6. What will be the result to those who overcome? Revelation 15:2

Lesson 22

1. Revelation 14:7	Saying with a l v, F G, a g g t h; f t h o h j i c: a w h t m h a e, a t s, a t f o w.
2. Revelation 14:8	And there f a a, s, B i f, i f, t g c, b s m a n d o t w o t w o h f.
3. Revelation 18:2	And he c m w a s v, s, B t g i f, i f, a i b t h o d, a t h o e f s, a a c o e u a h b.
4. Revelation 14:9–10	And the t a f t, s w a l v, I a m w t b a h i, a r h m i h f, o i h h, T s s d o t w o t w o G.
5. Revelation 14:12	Here is t p o t s: h a t t k t c o G, a t f o J.
6. Revelation 15:2	And I s a i w a s o g m w f: a t t h g t v o t b, a o h i, a o h m, a o t n o h n, s o t s o g, h t h o G.

THREE ANGELS' MESSAGES

51

23

SEVEN LAST PLAGUES

1. What is the first plague at the end time? Revelation 16:2

2. What are the second and third plagues? Revelation 16:3–4

3. What is the fourth plague? Revelation 16:8

4. What is the fifth plague? Revelation 16:10

5. Describe the sixth plague. Revelation 16:12

6. What takes place during the seventh plague? Revelation 16:17–18, 21

Lesson 23

1. Revelation 16:2	And the f w, a p o h v u t e; a t f a n a g s u t m w h t m o t b, a u t w w h i.
2. Revelation 16:3–4	And the s a p o h v u t s; a i b a t b o a d m: … And the t a p o h v u t r a f o w; a t b b.
3. Revelation 16:8	And the f a p o h v u t s; a p w g u h t s m w f.
4. Revelation 16:10	And the f a p o h v u t s o t b; a h k w f o d.
5. Revelation 16:12	And the s a p o h v u t g r E; a t w t w d u, t t w o t k o t e m b p
6. Revelation 16:17–18, 21	And the s a p o h v i t a; … a t w a g e, … A t f u m a g h o o h, e s a t w o a t: a m b G b o t p o t h; f t p t w e g.

SEVEN LAST PLAGUES

53

24
TRUST AND OBEY

1. What should we seek first? Matthew 6:33

2. What happens when we seek God? Matthew 7:7

3. What promise does Jesus give if we obey? John 14:14

4. Can we obey God through our own strength? Philippians 4:13

5. What can we do to overcome Satan? James 4:7

6. What is the result of obedience to God's commandments? Revelation 22:14

Lesson 24

1. Matthew 6:33	But seek y f t k o G, a h r; a a t t s b a u y.
2. Matthew 7:7	Ask, and i s b g y; s, a y s f; k, a i s b o u y.
3. John 14:14	If ye s a a t i m n, I w d i.
4. Philippians 4:13	I can d a t t C w s m.
5. James 4:7	Submit yourselves t t G. R t d, a h w f f y.
6. Revelation 22:14	Blessed are t t d H c, t t m h r t t t o l, a m e i t t g i t c.

TRUST AND OBEY

25

TRUE CHURCH

1. How is God's church described? Jeremiah 6:2

2. How is the pure woman (or church) described? Revelation 12:1

3. What kind of woman is described in Revelation 17:3?

4. Compare Revelation 17:3 to Revelation 12:17.

5. What is the testimony of Jesus? Revelation 19:10

6. What is God saying to you and me today? Revelation 18:4

Lesson 25

1. Jeremiah 6:2	I have l t d o Z t a c a d w.
2. Revelation 12:1	And there a a g w i h; a w c w t s, a t m u h f, a u h h a c o t s.
3. Revelation 17:3	So he c m a i t s i t w: a I s a w s u a s c b, f o n o b, h s h a t h.
4. Revelation 12:17	And the d w w w t w, a w t m w w t r o h s, w k t c o G, a h t t o J C.
5. Revelation 19:10	Worship God: f t t o J i t s o p.
6. Revelation 18:4	And I h a v f h, s, C o o h, m p, t y b n p o h s, a t y r n o h p.

BIBLE STUDY ANSWERS

Using the King James Version

1
Can We Trust The Bible?

1. **John 14:6**—Jesus saith unto him, <u>I am the way, the truth, and the life</u>; no man cometh unto the Father, but by me.

2. **John 17:17**—Sanctify them through thy truth, <u>thy word is truth</u>.

3. **2 Timothy 3:16**—<u>All scripture is given by inspiration of God</u>, and is profitable for doctrine, for reproof, for correction, for instruction in righteousness.

4. **2 Peter 1:21**—For the prophecy came not in old times by the will of man: but <u>holy men of God spake as they were moved by the Holy Ghost</u>.

5. **Psalm 119:11**—<u>Thy word have I hid in mine heart</u>, that I might not sin against Thee.

6. **Psalm 119:105**—Thy word <u>is a lamp unto my feet, and a light unto my path</u>.

2
Origin of Sin

1. **1 John 3:8**—He that committeth sin is of the devil; for <u>the devil sinneth from the beginning</u>.

2. **Isaiah 14:12-14**—How art thou fallen from heaven, O Lucifer, son of the morning! ... For thou hast said in thine heart ... <u>I will be like the most High</u>.

3. **Revelation 12:9**—<u>And the great dragon was cast out, that old serpent, called the Devil, and Satan,</u> which deceiveth the whole world: he was cast out into the earth, <u>and his angels were cast out with him</u>.

4. **1 John 3:4**—Whosoever committeth sin transgresseth also the law: for <u>sin is the transgression of the law</u>.

5. **Romans 3:23**—For <u>all have sinned</u>, and come short of the glory of God.

6. **John 3:16**—For God so loved the world, that he gave his only begotten Son, that <u>whosoever believeth in him should not perish, but have everlasting life</u>.

3
Salvation

1. **Acts 16:30**—And brought them out, and said, Sirs, <u>what must I do to be saved</u>?

2. **Acts 16:31**—And they said, <u>Believe on the Lord Jesus Christ, and thou shalt be saved</u>, and thy house.

3. **Romans 6:23**—For the wages of <u>sin is death;</u> but the <u>gift of God is eternal life</u> through Jesus Christ our Lord.

4. **1 John 1:9**—If we confess our sins, he is faithful and just to <u>forgive us our sins, and to cleanse us from all unrighteousness</u>.

5. **John 3:16**—For <u>God so loved the world</u>, that he gave his only begotten Son, that whosoever believeth in him should not perish, but have everlasting life.

6. **Revelation 3:20**—Behold, I stand at the door, and knock: if any man hear my voice, and <u>open the door</u>, I will come in to him, and will sup with him, and he with me.

4

Heaven And New Earth

1. **John 14:2-3**—<u>In my Father's house are many mansions</u>: if it were not so, I would have told you. <u>I go to prepare a place for you</u>. And if I go and prepare a place for you, I will come again, and receive you unto myself; that where I am, there ye may be also.

2. **1 Corinthians 2:9**—But as it is written, <u>Eye hath not seen, nor ear heard, neither have entered into the heart of man</u>, the things which God hath prepared for them that love Him.

3. **Revelation 21:2, 4**—And I John saw <u>the holy city, new Jerusalem, coming down from God out of heaven</u>, prepared as a bride adorned for her husband.... And God shall wipe away all tears from their eyes; and <u>there shall be no more death, neither sorrow, nor crying, neither shall there be any more pain</u>: for the former things are passed away.

4. **Revelation 22:2**—In the midst of the street of it, and on either side of the river, was there <u>the tree of life</u>, which bare twelve manner of fruits.

5. **Isaiah 65:21**—And they shall <u>build houses</u>, and inhabit them; and they shall <u>plant vineyards</u>, and eat the fruit of them.

6. **Revelation 22:14**—Blessed are <u>they that do his commandments</u>, that they may have right to the tree of life, and <u>may enter in through the gates into the city</u>.

5
God's Law

1. **Romans 7:12**—Wherefore <u>the law is holy, and the commandment holy, and just, and good</u>.

2. **Ecclesiastes 12:13**—Let us hear the conclusion of the whole matter: <u>Fear God, and keep His commandments</u>: for this is the whole duty of man.

3. **Matthew 5:17**—Think not that I am come to destroy the law, or the prophets: <u>I am not come to destroy, but to fulfill</u>.

4. **James 2:10**—For whosoever shall keep <u>the whole law</u>, and yet offend in one point, he is guilty of all.

5. **Psalm 111:7–8**—The works of His hands are verity and judgment; all His commandments are sure. <u>They stand fast forever and ever</u>, and are done in truth and uprightness.

6. **John 14:15**—If ye love me, <u>keep my commandments</u>.

6
Sabbath

1. **Genesis 2:3**—<u>And God blessed the seventh day, and sanctified it</u>: because that in it He had rested from all His work which God created and made.

2. **Exodus 20:8**—<u>Remember the sabbath day, to keep it holy</u>.

3. **Luke 4:16**—And he came to Nazareth, where he had been brought up: and, <u>as his custom was, he went into the synagogue on the sabbath day</u>, and stood up for to read.

4. **Luke 23:56**—And they returned, and prepared spices and ointments; and <u>rested the sabbath day</u> according to the commandment.

5. **Isaiah 66:23**—And it shall come to pass, that from one new moon to another, and <u>from one sabbath to another</u>, shall all flesh come to worship before me, saith the Lord.

6. **Mark 2:27-28**—And He said unto them, <u>The sabbath was made for man</u>, and not man for the sabbath: Therefore the Son of man is Lord also of the sabbath.

7
How to Keep the Sabbath

1. **Exodus 20:8–11**—<u>Remember the sabbath day, to keep it holy</u>. Six days shalt thou labour, and do all thy work: But the seventh day is the sabbath of the Lord thy God: in it <u>thou shalt not do any work</u>, thou, nor thy son, nor thy daughter, thy manservant, nor thy maidservant, nor thy cattle, nor thy stranger that is within thy gates: For in six days the Lord made heaven and earth, the sea, and all that in them is, and rested the seventh day: wherefore the Lord blessed the sabbath day, and hallowed it.

2. **Mark 15:42**—And now when the even was come, because it was <u>the preparation, that is, the day before the sabbath</u>.

3. **Genesis 1:5**—And <u>the evening and the morning</u> were the first day.

4. **Isaiah 58:13**—If thou turn away thy foot from the sabbath, from doing thy pleasure on my holy day; and call the sabbath a delight, the holy of the Lord, honourable; and shalt honour Him, <u>not doing thy own ways, nor finding thine own pleasure, nor speaking thine own words</u>.

5. **Matthew 12:12**—<u>Wherefore it is lawful to do well on the sabbath days</u>.

6. **Ezekiel 20:20**—And hallow <u>my sabbaths; and they shall be a sign between me and you</u>, that ye may know that I am the Lord your God.

8
First Day

1. **Matthew 28:1**—In the end of the sabbath, as it began to dawn <u>toward the first day of the week, came Mary Magdalene</u> and the other Mary to see the sepulchre.

2. **Mark 16:2**—And very early in the morning <u>the first day of the week, they came unto the sepulchre</u> at the rising of the sun.

3. **Luke 24:1**—Now upon <u>the first day of the week, very early in the morning, they came unto the sepulchre</u>, bringing the spices which they had prepared, and certain others with them.

4. **John 20:1**—<u>The first day of the week cometh Mary Magdalene early</u>, when it was yet dark, unto the sepulchre, and seeth the stone taken away from the sepulchre.

5. **Genesis 1:5**—And God called the light Day, and the darkness he called Night. And <u>the evening and the morning were the first day</u>.

6. **Matthew 15:9**—But in vain they do worship me, <u>teaching for doctrines the commandments of men</u>.

9

Signs of Jesus' Coming

1. **Matthew 24:7**—For <u>nation shall rise against nation</u>, and kingdom against kingdom: and there shall be <u>famines</u>, and <u>pestilences</u>, and <u>earthquakes</u>, in divers places.

2. **2 Timothy 3:2-3**—<u>For men shall be lovers of their own selves, covetous, boasters, proud, blasphemers, disobedient to parents, unthankful, unholy, Without natural affection, trucebreakers, false accusers, incontinent, fierce, despisers of those that are good</u>.

3. **Matthew 24:29**—Immediately after the tribulation of those days shall <u>the sun be darkened, and the moon shall not give her light, and the stars shall fall from heaven, and the powers of the heavens shall be shaken</u>.

4. **Matt. 24:21**—<u>For then shall be great tribulation, such as was not since the beginning of the world to this time, no, nor ever shall be</u>.

5. **Matthew 24:14**—And <u>this gospel of the kingdom shall be preached in all the world</u> for a witness unto all nations; and then shall the end come.

6. **Matthew 24:30**—And then <u>shall appear the sign of the Son of man in heaven</u>: and then shall all the tribes of the earth mourn, and <u>they shall see the Son of man coming in the clouds of heaven with power and great glory</u>.

10
Second Coming

1. **John 14:2-3**—In my Father's house are many mansions: If it were not so, I would have told you. I go to prepare a place for you. And if I go and prepare a place for you, <u>I will come again</u>, and receive you unto myself; that where I am, there ye may be also.

2. **Acts 1:11**—This same Jesus, which was taken up from you into heaven, <u>shall so come in like manner as ye have seen him go into heaven</u>.

3. **Revelation 1:7**—Behold, he cometh with clouds; and <u>every eye shall see him</u>.

4. **Matthew 24:44**—<u>Therefore be ye also ready</u>: for in such an hour as ye think not the Son of man cometh.

5. **Luke 21:28**—And when these things begin to come to pass, then <u>look up, and lift up your heads</u>; for your redemption draweth nigh. *{Note: Lift up your heads means to be joyful.}*

6. **Matthew 24:36**—But <u>of that day and hour knoweth no man</u>, no, not the angels of heaven, but my Father only.

11

Baptism

1. **Mark 16:16**—<u>He that believeth and is baptized shall be saved</u>; but he that believeth not shall be damned.

2. **Ephesians 4:5**—One Lord, one faith, <u>one baptism</u>.

3. **Acts 8:37-38**—And Philip said, If thou believest with all thine heart, thou mayest. And he answered and said, I believe that Jesus Christ is the Son of God. And he commanded the chariot to stand still: and they <u>went down both into the water, both Philip and the eunuch; and he baptized him</u>.

4. **Mark 1:9-11**—And it came to pass in those days, that Jesus came from Nazareth of Galilee, and was baptized of John in Jordan. And straightway <u>coming up out of the water</u>, he saw the heavens opened, and the Spirit like a dove descending upon Him. And there came a voice from heaven, saying, Thou art my beloved Son, in whom I am well pleased.

5. **1 Peter 2:21**—For even hereunto were ye called: because Christ also suffered for us, <u>leaving us an example</u>, that ye should follow His steps.

6. **Matthew 28:19-20**—Go ye therefore, and <u>teach all nations, baptizing them</u> in the name of the Father, and of the Son, and of the Holy Ghost: Teaching them to observe all things whatsoever I have commanded you: and lo, I am with you always, even unto the end of the world. Amen.

12

Prophecy

1. **Revelation 12:17**—And the dragon was wroth with the woman, and went to make war with the remnant of her seed, which keep the commandments of God, and have the testimony of Jesus Christ.

2. **Revelation 19:10**—And I fell at his feet to worship him. And he said unto me, See thou do it not: I am thy fellowservant, and of thy brethren that have the testimony of Jesus: worship God: for the testimony of Jesus is the spirit of prophecy.

3. **2 Peter 1:21**—For the prophecy came not in old time by the will of man: but holy men of God spake as they were moved by the Holy Ghost.

4. **Amos 3:7**—Surely the Lord God will do nothing, but He revealeth His secret unto His servants the prophets.

5. **Isaiah 8:20**—To the law and to the testimony: if they speak not according to this word, it is because there is no light in them.

6. **Acts 2:17**—And it shall come to pass in the last days, saith God, I will pour out of my Spirit upon all flesh: and your sons and your daughters shall prophesy, and your young men shall see visions, and your old men shall dream dreams.

13

Health

1. **Genesis 1:29**—And God said, Behold, I have given you every <u>herb bearing seed</u>, which is upon the face of all the earth, and every tree, in the which is <u>the fruit of a tree yielding seed</u>; to you it shall be for meat. *{fruits, nuts, and grains}*

2. **Genesis 3:18**—Thorns also and thistles shall it bring forth to thee; and thou shalt eat <u>the herb of the field</u>. *{vegetables}*

3. **Genesis 9:3**—<u>Every moving thing that liveth</u> shall be meat for you; even as the green herb have I given you all things. *{after the flood}*

4. **Genesis 7:2**—Of every <u>clean beast thou shalt take to thee by sevens</u>, the male and his female: and of <u>beasts that are not clean by two</u>, the male and his female.

5. **Deuteronomy 14:3, 6, 9**—Thou shalt not eat any abominable thing.... And every <u>beast that parteth the hoof, and cleaveth the cleft into two claws, and cheweth the cud</u> among the beasts, that ye shall eat.... These ye shall eat of all that are in the waters: <u>all that have fins and scales</u> shall ye eat.

6. **1 Corinthians 10:31**—Whether therefore ye eat, or drink, or whatsoever ye do, <u>do all to the glory of God</u>.

14
Tithes and Offerings

1. **Psalm 24:1**—<u>The earth is the Lord's</u>, and the fullness thereof; the world, and they that dwell therein.

2. **Matthew 6:20-21**—But <u>lay up for yourselves treasures in heaven</u>, where neither moth nor rust doth corrupt, and where thieves do not break through nor steal: For where your treasure is, there will your heart be also.

3. **Leviticus 27:32**—And concerning the tithe of the herd, or of the flock, even of whatsoever passeth under the rod, <u>the tenth</u> shall be holy unto the Lord.

4. **Malachi 3:10**—Bring ye all the tithes into the storehouse, that there may be meat in mine house, and prove me now herewith, saith the Lord of hosts, if I will not <u>open you the windows of heaven, and pour you out a blessing, that there shall not be room enough to receive it</u>.

5. **Psalm 96:8**—Give unto the Lord the glory due unto his name: <u>bring an offering</u>, and come into his courts.

6. **2 Corinthians 9:7**—Every man according as he purposeth in his heart, so let him give; not grudgingly, or of necessity: for <u>God loveth a cheerful giver</u>.

15

Sanctuary

1. **Exodus 25:8**—And let them make me a sanctuary; that I may dwell among them.

2. **Hebrews 9:2-3**—For there was a tabernacle made; the first, wherein was the candlestick, and the table, and the shewbread; which is called the sanctuary. And after the second veil, the tabernacle which is called the Holiest of all.

3. **Leviticus 4:29**—And he shall lay his hand upon the head of the sin offering, and slay the sin offering in the place of the burnt offering.

4. **John 1:29**—The next day John seeth Jesus coming unto him, and saith, Behold the Lamb of God, which taketh away the sin of the world.

5. **Hebrews 9:24**—For Christ is not entered into the holy places made with hands, which are the figures of the true; but into heaven itself, now to appear in the presence of God for us.

6. **Acts 4:12**—Neither is there salvation in any other: for there is none other name under heaven given among men, whereby we must be saved. {*Jesus*}

16

Judgment

1. **Ecclesiastes 3:17**—I said in mine heart, God shall judge <u>the righteous and the wicked</u>: for there is a time there for every purpose and for every work.

2. **Ecclesiastes 12:14**—For <u>God shall bring every work into judgment</u>, with every secret thing, whether it be good, or whether it be evil.

3. **Revelation 20:12**—And I saw the dead, small and great, stand before God; and <u>the books</u> were opened: and another book was opened, which is <u>the book of life</u>: and the dead were judged out of those things which were written in the books, according to their works.

4. **2 Corinthians 5:10**—For we must <u>all</u> appear before the judgment seat of Christ.

5. **Romans 14:12**—So then <u>every one of us shall give account of himself to God</u>.

6. **Revelation 22:12**—And, behold, I come quickly; and my reward is with me, to give every man <u>according as his work shall be</u>.

17
Church Standards

1. **Philippians 4:8**—Finally, brethren, <u>whatsoever things are true</u>, whatsoever things are <u>honest</u>, whatsoever things are <u>just</u>, whatsoever things are <u>pure</u>, whatsoever things are <u>lovely</u>, whatsoever things are of <u>good report</u>; <u>if there be any virtue</u>, and <u>if there be any praise</u>, think on these things.

2. **1 Corinthians 10:31**—Whether therefore ye eat, or drink, or whatsoever ye do, <u>do all to the glory of God</u>.

3. **Ephesians 4:31–32**—<u>Let all bitterness, and wrath, and anger, and clamour, and evil speaking, be put away from you</u>, with all malice: And <u>be ye kind one to another, tenderhearted, forgiving one another</u>, even as God for Christ's sake hath forgiven you.

4. **Ephesians 5:4**—Neither filthiness, <u>nor foolish talking</u>, nor jesting, which are not convenient: but rather giving of thanks.

5. **Romans 12:2**—And <u>be not conformed to this world</u>: but be ye transformed by the renewing of your mind, that ye may prove what is that good, and acceptable, and perfect, will of God.

6. **1 Peter 3:3**—<u>Whose adorning let it not be that outward adorning of plaiting the hair, and of wearing of gold, or of putting on of apparel</u>. *{Dress modestly}*

18
Death

1. **Genesis 2:17**—<u>But of the tree of the knowledge of good and evil, thou shalt not eat of it</u>: for in the day that thou eatest thereof thou shalt surely die.

2. **Genesis 3:4**—And the serpent said unto the woman, <u>Ye shall not surely die</u>.

3. **Ecclesiastes 12:7**—Then shall <u>the dust return to the earth</u> as it was: and the <u>spirit shall return unto God</u> who gave it.

4. **Job 27:3**—All the while my <u>breath</u> is in me, and the spirit of God is in my nostrils.

5. **Genesis 2:7**—And the Lord God formed man of the <u>dust</u> of the ground, and <u>breathed</u> into his nostrils the breath of life; and man became a living soul. *{Dust + Breath = Living Soul}*

6. **John 5:28–29**—Marvel not at this: for the hour is coming, in the <u>which all that are in the graves shall hear his voice. And shall come forth</u>; they that have done good, unto the resurrection of life; and they that have done evil, unto the resurrection of damnation.

19

1,000 Years

1. **Revelation 20:1-2**—And I saw an angel come down from heaven, having the key of the bottomless pit and a great chain in his hand. And <u>he laid hold on the dragon, that old serpent, which is the Devil, and Satan, and bound him a thousand years</u>.

2. **Revelation 20:6**—Blessed and holy is he that hath part in the first resurrection: on such the second death hath no power, <u>but they shall be priests of God and of Christ, and shall reign with him a thousand years</u>.

3. **Revelation 20:4**—And I saw thrones, and they sat upon them, and <u>judgment was given unto them</u> ... and they lived and reigned with Christ a thousand years.

4. **Jeremiah 4:23**—I beheld <u>the earth, and, lo, it was without form, and void</u>; and the heavens, and they had no light.

5. **Revelation 20:7, 10**—And when the thousand years are expired, Satan shall be loosed out of his prison,... <u>And the devil that deceived them was cast into the lake of fire and brimstone</u>.

6. **Revelation 21:4**—And God shall wipe away all tears from their eyes; and <u>there shall be no more death, neither sorrow, nor crying, neither shall there be any more pain</u>: for the former things are passed away.

20

The Little Horn

1. **Daniel 7:4**—*First beast*: The first was like <u>a lion</u>, and had eagle's wings. *Second beast*: And behold another beast, a second, like to <u>a bear</u>. *Third beast*: After this I beheld, and lo another, like <u>a leopard</u>. *Fourth beast*: After this I saw in the night visions, and behold a fourth beast, <u>dreadful and terrible</u>, and strong exceedingly; and it had great iron teeth.

2. **Daniel 7:17**—These great beasts, which are four, are four <u>kings</u>, which shall arise out of the earth. {kings or kingdoms}

3. **Daniel 7:8**—I considered the horns, and, behold, there came up among them another little horn ... and, behold, in this horn were eyes like the eyes of man, and <u>a mouth speaking great things</u>.

4. **Mark 2:7**—Why doth this man thus speak <u>blasphemies</u>? <u>who can forgive sins but God only</u>?

5. **John 10:33**—The Jews answered him, saying, For a good work we stone thee not; but for <u>blasphemy</u>; and because that <u>thou, being a man, makest thyself God</u>.

6. **Daniel 7:25**—And he shall speak great words against the most High, and shall wear out the saints of the most High, and <u>think to change times and laws</u>: and they shall be given into his hand until a time and times and the dividing of time.

21

Mark of the Beast

1. **Exodus 20:8, 11**—Remember the sabbath day, to keep it holy.... For in six days <u>the Lord made heaven and earth, the sea</u>, and all that in them is, and rested the seventh day: wherefore the Lord blessed the sabbath day, and hallowed it. *{Seal contains: Name [Lord], Title [creator], & Territory [heaven, earth, and sea]}*

2. **Exodus 31:17**—<u>It is a sign between me and the children of Israel</u> for ever: for in six days the Lord made heaven and earth, and on the seventh day he rested, and was refreshed.

3. **Galatians 3:26, 29**—For <u>ye are all the children of God by faith in Christ Jesus</u>.... And <u>if ye be Christ's, then are ye Abraham's seed</u>, and heirs according to the promise.

4. **Revelation 12:17**—And the <u>dragon</u> *{Satan}* was wroth with the <u>woman</u> *{God's church}*, and went to make war with the remnant of her seed, which keep the commandments of God, and have the testimony of Jesus Christ.

5. **Revelation 13:2**—And the beast which I saw was <u>like unto a leopard, and his feet were as the feet of a bear, and his mouth as the mouth of a lion: and the dragon gave him his power, and his seat, and great authority</u>.

6. **Revelation 13:16**—And he causeth all, both small and great, rich and poor, free and bond, to receive <u>a mark in their right hand, or in their foreheads</u>.

22
Three Angels' Messages

1. **Revelation 14:7**—Saying with a loud voice, <u>Fear God, and give glory to him; for the hour of his judgment is come: and worship him that made heaven, and earth, and the sea</u>, and the fountains of waters.

2. **Revelation 14:8**—And there followed another angel, saying, <u>Babylon is fallen</u>, is fallen, that great city, because she made all nations drink of the wine of the wrath of her fornication.

3. **Revelation 18:2**—And he cried mightily with a strong voice, saying, Babylon the great is fallen, is fallen, and is become <u>the habitation of devils, and the hold of every foul spirit, and a cage of every unclean and hateful bird</u>.

4. **Revelation 14:9-10**—And the third angel followed them, saying with a loud voice, <u>If any man worship the beast and his image, and receive his mark in his forehead, or in his hand, The same shall drink of the wine of the wrath of God</u>.

5. **Revelation 14:12**—Here is the patience of the saints: here are <u>they that keep the commandments of God, and the faith of Jesus</u>.

6. **Revelation 15:2**—And I saw as it were a sea of glass mingled with fire: and <u>them that had gotten the victory over the beast, and over his image, and over his mark, and over the number of his name, stand on the sea of glass, having the harps of God</u>.

23

Seven Last Plagues

1. **Revelation 16:2**—And the first went, and poured out his vial upon the earth; and there fell <u>a noisome and grievous sore upon the men which had the mark of the beast, and upon them which worshipped his image</u>.

2. **Revelation 16:3-4**—And the second angel poured out his vial upon <u>the sea; and it became as the blood of a dead man</u> ... And the third angel poured out his vial upon the <u>rivers and fountains of waters; and they became blood</u>.

3. **Revelation 16:8**—And the fourth angel poured out his vial upon <u>the sun; and power was given unto him to scorch men with fire</u>.

4. **Revelation 16:10**—And the fifth angel poured out his vial upon the <u>seat of the beast; and his kingdom was full of darkness</u>.

5. **Revelation 16:12**—And the sixth angel poured out his vial upon <u>the great river Euphrates; and the water thereof was dried up</u>, that the way of the kings of the east might be prepared.

6. **Revelation 16:17, 18, 21**—And the seventh angel poured out his vial into the air; ... and <u>there was a great earthquake</u>, ... And <u>there fell upon men a great hail out of heaven, every stone about the weight of a talent</u>: and men blasphemed God because of the plague of the hail; for the plague thereof was exceeding great.

24

Trust And Obey

1. **Matthew 6:33**—But seek ye first <u>the kingdom of God</u>, and <u>his righteousness</u>; and all these things shall be added unto you.

2. **Matthew 7:7**—<u>Ask, and it shall be given you; seek, and ye shall find; knock, and it shall be opened unto you.</u>

3. **John 14:14**—If ye shall <u>ask any thing in my name, I will do it</u>.

4. **Philippians 4:13**—<u>I can do all things through Christ</u> which strengtheneth me.

5. **James 4:7**—<u>Submit yourselves therefore to God. Resist the devil</u>, and he will flee from you.

6. **Revelation 22:14**—Blessed are they that do his commandments, <u>that they may have right to the tree of life, and may enter in through the gates into the city</u>.

25
True Church

1. **Jeremiah 6:2**—I have likened the daughter of Zion to a comely and delicate <u>woman</u>. *{Woman = Church}*

2. **Revelation 12:1**—And there appeared a great wonder in heaven; <u>a woman clothed with the sun, and the moon under her feet</u>, and <u>upon her head a crown of twelve stars</u>.

3. **Revelation 17:3**—So he carried me away in the spirit into the wilderness: and I saw <u>a woman sit upon a scarlet coloured beast, full of names of blasphemy</u>, having seven heads and ten horns.

4. **Revelation 12:17**—And the dragon was wroth with the woman, and went to make war with the remnant of her seed, which <u>keep the commandments of God</u>, <u>and have the testimony of Jesus Christ</u>.

5. **Revelation 19:10**—Worship God: for <u>the testimony of Jesus is the spirit of prophecy</u>.

6. **Revelation 18:4**—And I heard another voice from heaven, saying, <u>Come out of her, my people</u>, that ye be not partakers of her sins, and that ye receive not of her plagues.

We invite you to view the complete
selection of titles we publish at:
www.TEACHServices.com

We encourage you to write us
with your thoughts about this,
or any other book we publish at:
info@TEACHServices.com

TEACH Services' titles may be purchased in
bulk quantities for educational, fund-raising,
business, or promotional use.
bulksales@TEACHServices.com

Finally, if you are interested in seeing
your own book in print, please contact us at:
publishing@TEACHServices.com

We are happy to review your manuscript at no charge.

www.ingramcontent.com/pod-product-compliance
Lightning Source LLC
Chambersburg PA
CBHW080524110426
42742CB00017B/3226